Vice-Chancellor, Ladies and Gentlemen,

Among the many events which have conspired to make this pleasant occasion possible, I should like to single out two in particular. The first is the establishment of the Chair of Medieval and Renaissance English and the installation of C. S. Lewis as its first holder in 1954. It was Lewis's writings that first made me – as they have made so many others – into a medievalist, and it is with a special pleasure, and a special sense of privilege, that I find myself following in his footsteps. What I particularly admire in Lewis is not only the honesty of his responses to literature and the unpretentious clarity that makes his works accessible even to unsophisticated schoolgirls in the North-East of England, but also his refusal to confine his literary interests within the limits of Middle English; he was as at home with works in Latin, French and Italian as with literature in the native tongue. This European perspective is also characteristic of his successors in the Chair, Jack Bennett and John Stevens, and it is, I think, a special strength of medieval studies in Cambridge, where medievalists form a kind of academic freemasonry of fellowship and mutual support that knows no bounds of Faculty or Department. My ambition would be to keep this tradition flourishing, with the generous support of my colleagues in other disciplines which I have come to expect. In the European climate of the 1990s, we may hope that medievalists have a new role opening up for them, as the period when literature crossed national boundaries in sublime disregard of linguistic barriers comes to have a new relevance. The second event I should like to mention is the admission of women as full members of the University in 1948, because I think this a fitting moment to record my gratitude to and admiration for the women and men who worked to make it possible. It is always a matter of wonderment to me how recent this event is – less than fifty years have passed – and I am very conscious of my good fortune in living at a time when I can enjoy the freedoms so laboriously won.[1] If it is not actually true to say that I had *no* disadvantages by virtue of being a woman (as indeed it would still not be true of a woman today), still I cannot but be conscious that a path was opened up for me, and I must hope that it will be wider and even smoother for those coming after me.

My subject today, however, is not the status of women in this university, but rather one particular aspect of their status in medieval literature, which will, I hope, illuminate the possibilities for dialogue between that literature and the present – dialogue in the sense that if we interrogate it in the light of our own concerns, we may, paradoxically, allow it to speak to us with its own voice in ways it has never been allowed to before.[2]

Eric Segal's *Love Story*, a book which was turned into a very successful film, contains the famous line: 'Love means not ever having to say you're sorry.' If this maxim is true, then it would seem that medieval writers didn't love women very much, because they are constantly apologising to them. They apologise to women for two things in particular: first of all, for using bad language, for failing to disguise references to sexuality under a modest cloak of euphemism. Second, they apologise for making misogynistic remarks, or for presenting an unflattering picture of the female sex. Of course, such apologies are few and far between when set against the monstrous bulk of antifeminist literature in the Middle Ages, which constitutes a whole genre by itself.[3] But we may well ask why they exist at all. Antifeminism is so massive a presence in the medieval literary scene, so much an accepted part of literary convention, that one wonders why writers bothered to apologise for it. Are these apologies themselves as conventional as the antifeminism for which they purportedly attempt reparation? Or, to put the question the other way round, are we ever licensed to take them at face value, as evidence of a genuine sensitivity to what real-life women might be thinking and feeling? These questions were originally prompted by my instinctive assumption that when Chaucer apologises to women, we *are* justified in supposing that a concern for real-life women is manifesting itself one way or another, and it is this assumption that I want to test against the larger background of medieval literature.

I shall begin with the more specific apologies for bad language, since they are less numerous, and then widen the investigation to the more general apologies for speaking ill of women. An example of the first sort appears at the end of Boccaccio's *Decameron* – a work which is not habitually thought of as 'women's fiction', but which Boccaccio explicitly tells us in the Preface to the work was written to provide support and solace for ladies, particularly those who are in love, and do not have the same opportunities for distraction in physical activity that men have. At the opening of Day Four, Boccaccio again addresses his audience as 'dearest ladies', and reports that he has come under attack for taking 'so much delight in entertaining and consoling you, and ... in singing your praises as I do'.[4] He justifies himself by telling a story about a Florentine citizen called Filippo Balducci, a widower who had brought up his only son from early infancy while living the life of a hermit

3

in a cave outside the city. When the boy reached the age of eighteen, Filippo finally judged that his attachment to the service of God was so great that he could risk taking him in to Florence on one of his periodic trips to buy provisions. The young man was amazed at his first sight of the city – the palaces, houses and churches – but was particularly transfixed by the sight of a group of young women passing in the street. Never having seen a woman before, he asked his father what these beautiful creatures were. Not wishing to arouse any improper desires in his son, Filippo answered 'They are called goslings' ('Elle si chiamano papere'). This diversionary tactic proved a failure, however: the son, henceforth oblivious to all the other attractions of the city, begged his father to get him 'one of those goslings'. In vain did his father assure him that goslings are evil creatures; he insisted that he had never seen anything so angelic in his life. 'O alas! if you have any concern for my welfare, do make it possible for us to take one of those goslings back, and I will pop things into its bill.'[5] So, Boccaccio concludes, if a young man who had never set eyes on a woman was so instantly captivated by feminine charm, why should anyone reproach *him* for being enslaved by the grace and beauty of women?

It turns out to be no accident that Boccaccio uses this story about the attempt to circumvent natural sexual desires by a linguistic disguise in order to emphasise his relation to his female audience. For when, at the end of the whole work, he apologises to this female audience for having 'sometimes caused ladies to say, and very often to hear, things which are not suitable to be heard or said by virtuous women' in the course of the work, he appeals to euphemism for his defence: nothing is so unseemly as to prevent anyone from mentioning it, provided it is referred to in seemly lan-

4

guage.[6] So, given that there is nothing improper in men and women using such words as 'hole', 'rod', 'mortar', 'pestle', 'crumpet' and 'stuffing' in their everyday speech, there is nothing improper, Boccaccio says, in his having introduced similar terms into his narratives.[7] Yet the story about the goslings seems to indicate the conscious inadequacy of this defence: it doesn't matter what a thing is called; sexual desire is not eradicated by linguistic variation. Indeed, it is the linguistic variation that constitutes the excitement of the 'gosling' story. The young man's innocence allows him the licence of naming his desires directly – or what *he* thinks is directly – but it also denies him the knowledge of what those desires truly are; the reader's enjoyment of the story lies in decoding not only the father's euphemism but also the young man's innocent directness; sexuality is cloaked and revealed at the same time. Boccaccio's final apology similarly uses the question of female delicacy or prudery to imcrease the reader's enjoyment of linguistic displacement; it seems improbable that it was seriously prompted by concern for his women readers.

This does not mean that real-life women were not offended by crude language and innuendo alike. At the beginning of the fifteenth century we find Christine de Pisan, herself an author of some celebrity, objecting to the *Romance of the Rose*, and especially the part of it written by Jean de Meun, not only for its antifeminist passages, but also because of its use of improper language:[8] the prime example occurs when the personification Reason, in making passing mention of the myth of the castration of Saturn, refers in plain terms to the god's testicles ('coilles': 5507).[9] Like learned counsel asking the jury in the trial of *Lady Chatterley's Lover* whether they would give the book to their

5

children, wives or servants,[10] Christine asks the defenders of the *Rose* if they would let their daughters read it; it is, she says, a work that could not be read in public without bringing a blush to the cheeks of queens, princesses and other noble ladies.[11]

What is interesting is that Christine's objection is already anticipated in the *Romance of the Rose* itself. The Lover, the central figure of the poem, whom Reason is trying to dissuade from vain human love in favour of the love of God, likewise takes exception to her use of the word 'coilles'. What is even more interesting is that he objects to it precisely because, he says, it is an improper word to hear on the lips of a well-bred young lady ('cortaise pucele'); she ought to have glossed the term by using some polite word ('cortaise parole': 6898–906). The apology which we might expect to find made *to* a woman is here demanded *from* a woman, and one can sense Jean de Meun's enjoyment of the comedy in this reversal, as the Lover tries to make Reason, daughter of God, conform to his notion of blushing femininity.[12] Reason mounts a serious defence: there is nothing shameful about naming the male genitals, she says, which were created by God himself in paradise, for the noble end of perpetuating the human race. God may have made the things, says the Lover, but he didn't make the words. No, says Reason, he delegated the power of naming to her, and there is nothing base in the words: if testicles were called 'relics', and relics, 'testicles' no doubt the Lover would find 'relics' a dirty word. It's true, she says, that women customarily use euphemisms such as 'purses, harness, thingies' and so on ('borses, harnais, riens, piches, pines') – but they don't have any aversion to the *things* denoted by these terms, only to their plain names (6913–7122).[13]

Over one hundred years later, Christine de Pisan and the defenders of the *Rose* vigorously rehearse these same arguments (without seeming to notice that they already form part of the text itself) – only, in the real-life debate, the male and female roles are reversed. It is Christine who on behalf of her sex demands an apology for bad language from the admirers of the work – and fails to get it. She agrees that it is the bodily parts themselves, and not the words that denote them, that are improper, but she thinks the best course is not to name them at all, either directly or euphemistically;[14] to mention 'testicles' to a lover, she says, can only have an inflammatory effect (given that the word occurs in a story about castration, this seems to me rather an odd idea).[15] Her one supporter, Jean Gerson, chancellor of the University of Paris, likewise argued that the open reference to sexual matters stimulates sexual desire.[16] But when Pierre Col, canon of Paris and Tournai, defended Jean de Meun by saying that outside of the offending passage, he uses euphemisms for sexual subjects,[17] Christine replied – accurately but somewhat inconsistently – that these euphemisms are even *more* inflammatory than the use of plain terms would be.[18]

The ending of the *Romance of the Rose*, which describes the sexual consummation of the Lover's desire, is indeed a triumph of euphemism. The sexual act is described entirely in terms of a metaphorical pilgrimage to a religious shrine; the reversal of religious and sexual language hypothesised by Reason here becomes a reality.[19] Armed with his pilgrim's staff and the bulging wallet which hangs from it, the Lover falls to his knees before the sanctuary, a hidden recess supported on two silver pillars, and despite the narrowness of the aperture, he gradually works his way inside. Maureen

Quilligan has argued that this elaborately developed meta-phor is Jean de Meun's way of showing what courtly euphemism does to allegory: true allegory, she says, reveals multiple meaning in *things*, as Reason wistfully points out to the Lover that her direct naming of Saturn's testicles was intended to lead to a revelation of deeper meaning in the legend (7128–54). But the unveiling of the hidden meaning in euphemism, Quilligan says, reveals nothing but 'the carnal, the merely erotic'. 'Lifting the veil of such metaphor-ical language is simply to lift up skirts, to discover physical objects only.'[20] She is right, I think, as far as allegory is concerned. But the death of allegory is, one might say, the birth of sexuality. Allegory here reduces itself to a kind of linguistic striptease; the peeling off of euphemism generates excitement and desire by virtue of the introduction of delay and displacement. Sex is transformed into sexuality when it is no longer simply a physical act, but when it 'happens in the head' – when it becomes something that human beings *represent* to themselves. The excitement is produced not so much by what the Lover is doing, as by the disjunction between language and action which creates the sense of sexual play.

Euphemism plays a crucial role in the displacement of sex from the physical to the mental plane. Howard Bloch's study of the Old French fabliaux suggests it has the same function there: 'the dismemberment of meaning becomes the source of sexual desire ... linguistic gaps or differences ... are the source of the theme of erotic longing'.[21] And again female delicacy about direct naming of sexual matters is given a role to play. The classic example is the fabliau story of the maiden who could not hear any direct talk of sex without becoming 'sick to her stomach'.[22] A sharp young man called

David pretends to be just as sensitive to such talk as she is, and ends up in bed with her, her father assuming that nothing can happen between such milksops. But it turns out to be only the *words* that the girl objects to; she is quite happy to enter into sexual activity so long as it is represented as something else. As David explores each part of her body in turn, she supplies her own glosses: 'this is', she says, 'my meadow, and the hollow in the middle of it is my freshwater spring' (141–9); exploring David's body in her turn, she finds that he has a fine 'horse', with two 'grooms' to look after it, but, David tells her, it has had nothing to eat since the day before (173–87). With a flash of inspiration, linguistic consummation is achieved: 'David', she says, 'why don't you put your horse to graze in my meadow ...' (188–9).

Female sensitivity to rude words is thus invoked – indeed, is probably created – as a means of distinguishing levels of language, and consequently creating a crucial area of play in the gap between words and things, an area where both romantic delicacy and sexual fantasy can establish themselves. And the apologies to women are merely a strategy for drawing attention to these different linguistic levels, the possible ways of talking about the same things, and of attaching excitement and tension to the choice of one or the other.

When Chaucer apologises to women for uncouth language, at the end of the *Merchant's Tale*, the apology thus appropriately comes as the climax of a tale which seems to play itself out at two linguistic levels. But the apology works in the opposite direction from Boccaccio's; it does not signal the covert enjoyment of the forbidden, but rather the abrupt abandonment of linguistic illusion. It turns both sexuality and romance back into simple sex. The *Merchant's Tale* is

9

about a repulsive old knight called January, who suddenly decides to get married after a long life of lecherous bachelorhood. His meditations on the charms of his young bride May take the form of the romantic clichés traditionally used by medieval poets to conjure up a picture of feminine perfection:

> Hir fresshe beautee and hir age tendre,
> Hir myddel smal, hire armes longe and sklendre,
> Hir wise governaunce, hir gentillesse,
> Hir wommanly berynge, and hire sadnesse.   (1601–4)[23]

Her beautiful appearance at her wedding feast calls forth flights of poetic rapture: it seems an enchantment ('fayerye'); Queen Esther never looked so meekly on Ahasuerus; she is 'lyk the brighte morwe of May / Fulfild of alle beautee and plesaunce' (1742–9). Not surprisingly, the sight of her kindles an instant passion in January's young squire Damian, who in true romantic fashion almost swoons with the power of his feelings, and straightway takes to his bed, weeping and lamenting. But when he manages to make his passion known to May by secretly pressing a letter into her hand, this romantic picture begins to dissolve. In order to read this letter in secret, May pretends to have to go to the privy – or, as the narrator euphemistically puts it, she goes 'Ther as ye woot that every wight moot nede' (1951). The specifics of the narrative soon make it necessary to name this unromantic location directly, however: when May has read this letter carefully, she tears it into tiny pieces and throws it, the narrator says, 'in the pryvee' (1954). The shift from euphemism to plain naming marks a shift in our view of May. The unsentimental efficiency she exhibits here turns out to characterise all her subsequent arrangements to satisfy Damian's desires – and of course her own, both of them turning out to be physical desires only. The sweet romantic heroine, whom we have been willing to see as a tender young victim of her old husband's senile appetites, turns out to be a hard-headed manipulator of people and events, so that the narrator's continued use of a romantic vocabulary – 'This gentil May, fulfilled of pitee' (1995; cf. 2328) – seems more and more at odds with the events of the narrative. The linguistic breaking-point comes when May and Damian are about to consum-mate their desires in – of all places – a pear-tree. January, by now blind, and excessively jealous, insists on keeping his hand on his wife at all times, but he is persuaded to let her climb into the pear-tree to pick a pear while he encircles its trunk with his arms to prevent anyone following – unaware that Damian, by pre-arrangement, is already waiting in the tree. At this point the narrator's ability to describe what is going on in polite language momentarily gives way: stand-ing on her blind husband's back, May catches hold of a branch,

> ... and up she gooth –
> Ladyes, I prey yow that ye be nat wrooth;
> I kan nat glose, I am a rude man –
> And sodeynly anon this Damyan
> Gan pullen up the smok, and in he throng.   (2349–53)

Given a little time, however, the narrator recovers himself, and does better when he has to describe January, his sight suddenly restored to him by a miracle, taking in what is going on over his head.

> Up to the tree he caste his eyen two,
> And saugh that Damyan his wyf had dressed

> In swich manere it may nat been expressed,
> But if I wolde speke uncurteisly.   (2360–3)

One thinks at first that he is about to repeat his earlier crudity, but with a superb linguistic swerve he veers aside into the safety of circumlocution.

The apology to 'ladies' for the temporary loss of courteous language here seems particularly ludicrous in view of the glaringly *un*courteous example of female behaviour which is its subject-matter. And that, of course, must be Chaucer's point. The patronising protectiveness which would herd women into a linguistic ghetto is revealed as nothing more than a piece of masculine naivety;[24] like Jean de Meun, Chaucer sees the fiction of female delicacy as a necessary ingredient in masculine romantic illusion.[25] In fact, the *Merchant's Tale* suggests, it is not women whom such language insulates from reality, but men. The romantic veil of illusion which January has thrown over his wife is not decisively rent even by this devastating moment of revelation. His physical blindness is cured by a miracle, but his spiritual blindness does duty for it: May manages to persuade him that his eyes were deceiving him and that what he plainly saw never took place. The *Merchant's Tale* suggests that women fittingly use the cloak of illusion which courtly language throws around them as a cover behind which they can get their own way.

The apologies to women for bad language are therefore more than a simple bow to prevailing social convention; they are the key to a whole nexus of attitudes to sexuality and language. What about the second category of apologies I mentioned, the cases where writers make antifeminist remarks and then apologise for them? Are they too merely a literary strategy, in which women are a pretext for addressing other concerns? Or do they show a genuine sensitivity to women as literary subjects and audience? We may begin with Jean de Meun, who again anticipates Christine de Pisan's criticisms of the *Romance of the Rose*, this time for antifeminism, by using a suitable lull in his narrative to apologise both to women and to members of the religious orders for the unflattering images of themselves that they might find in his work. It is not, he says, that he harbours anger or resentment against any woman alive; to despise women is the sign of an evil nature. His aim was simply the disinterested pursuit of knowledge. If it seems to his female readers that he is telling untruths, he advises them to direct their indignation not against him, but against his literary sources, the 'aucteurs' whose words he is simply repeating. They were experts in female behaviour; he merely reproduces what they said, with, perhaps, some slight verbal variation of the sort poets are licensed to make (15165–212). In one sense, Jean de Meun's apology seems unnecessary: he makes no antifeminist comments in his own voice, and, as the defenders of the *Rose* point out to Christine, the worst remarks of this kind are put into the mouth of a Jealous Husband, whose behaviour is explicitly offered to the Lover as an example of how he should *not* behave towards women (9391–412).[26] This defence however cut no ice with Christine de Pisan, who claimed to know of a woman whose husband read the *Romance of the Rose* aloud to her, showering her with blows all the while and crying 'This wise man Jean de Meun knew well what women were capable of!'[27] As for Jean's excuse that he is only quoting others, she answers that the repetition of a slander increases the evil.

Whatever one thinks of the merits of the literary-critical arguments produced by those involved in what is known as 'the quarrel of the *Rose*', it is true that Jean de Meun's protestation of innocence in his apology itself raises the suspicion of guilt by seeming deliberately to flaunt the antifeminist material in his work.[28] Certainly we are entitled to doubt the sincerity of other apologies of this sort. The earliest of them that I know of occurs in the *Roman de Troie* of Benoît de Sainte-Maure, written around 1165.[29] This long poetic version of the story of Troy contains much material invented by Benoît himself, not the least important of which is the earliest outline of the story of Troilus and Cressida, although the heroine is at this stage called Briseida. Describing Briseida's grief at her enforced departure from Troy and Troilus to join her father in the Greek camp, Benoît anticipates her future treachery in abandoning Troilus for Diomede, and seizes the opportunity for some acid comments on female fickleness. A woman's grief, he says, doesn't last long; if she weeps with one eye, she laughs with the other. The wisest of them is a giddy thing; she will take three days to forget someone she has loved for seven years. What is more, you can't criticise them for it; they all think their behaviour is perfectly justifiable (13441–56).Then, however, he adds that he fears he will be blamed for these remarks by the noble lady of a noble king ('Riche dame de riche rei'), who is the very epitome of goodness, generosity, beauty and other virtues, and for whom he wishes eternal good fortune. As Solomon said, whoever finds a good woman should praise God for it (13457–91). Who this 'riche dame' is, scholars are not entirely certain, but it seems likely that she is Eleanor of Aquitaine, wife of King Henry II of England; the *Roman de Troie* was probably composed for the royal pair. At any rate, the direct address to her fits in with Benoît's habit of addressing his audience as if speaking to them directly – a habit which, it has been claimed recently, marked a new kind of narrative, contrasting with the earlier impersonal mode of such works as the *Song of Roland*.[30] Chaucer's *Troilus and Criseyde* shows us this kind of personalised narrative, in which author and audience are made part of the very substance of the text, in fully developed form; he constantly addresses his readers as if they were a listening audience, identifying now one section of it and now another. At the opening of his poem he speaks to lovers; at its close he speaks to women, apologising for the anti-feminist implications of his story. The apologies to women can thus be seen as a by-product of the poet's wish to dramatise his relationship with his audience, as Boccaccio dramatises his relationship with the 'dearest ladies'.[31]

True as this may be, is it the whole truth about Chaucer's *Troilus and Criseyde?* When Boccaccio turned the scattered series of episodes in which Benoît relates Troilus's unhappy love-affair into a full-length autonomous narrative, he had no compunction in drawing antifeminist conclusions from it – 'A young woman is fickle and desirous of many lovers' – and he does not even attempt to mitigate them with any apologies.[32] But Chaucer included such an apology even though he not only omitted all antifeminist comment but also made Criseyde a much more complex and sympathetic figure. When obliged to relate Criseyde's unfaithfulness, he protests his unwillingness to 'chide' her; merely retelling her story is punishment enough, and if he could, he would excuse her for pity – 'I wolde excuse hire yet for routhe' (v 1093–9). At the end of his work, he asks the women in his audience not to take offence at what he has had to relate of one of their sex, beseeching

> every lady bright of hewe,
> And every gentil womman, what she be,
> That al be that Criseyde was untrewe,
> That for that gilt she be nat wroth with me.
> Ye may hire gilt in othere bokes se;
> And gladlier I wol write, yif yow leste,
> Penelopeës trouthe and good Alceste.   (v 1772–8)

Well, Christine de Pisan might say, why didn't you do that in the first place? I think there are good reasons to account for Chaucer having told this story of female unfaithfulness without making it necessary to convict him of bias against women,[33] but this is a larger subject which would lead me too far away from my present topic. As far as the apology is concerned, Chaucer at least made good his protestation that he would rather write about such good women as Penelope and Alcestis, by taking them as the literary subject of a work which is explicitly offered as reparation for the *Troilus*. The *Legend of Good Women* begins with a long Prologue which shows Chaucer being soundly ticked off by the God of Love for having translated the *Romance of the Rose*, which is a heresy against his law, and for having written *Troilus and Criseyde*, which, he says, shows women in a bad light and makes men mistrustful of them (F332–5; G 264–6). Chaucer's use of Jean de Meun's excuse in his earlier apology – that Criseyde's guilt is already on record in 'othere bokes' – is contemptuously dismissed: Chaucer himself, the God says, has at least sixty books which contain lots of stories about women who were 'goode and trewe'; why couldn't he have chosen to repeat some of them? Chaucer is rescued from the God of Love's anger by his female consort, who turns out to be Alcestis herself, and who defends Chaucer on the rather unflattering grounds that he perhaps just translated his narratives in a routine way, without giving much thought to their content (F 362–5; G 340–3). She imposes on him as penance for his fault the composition of 'a glorious legende / Of goode wymmen' – a story-collection relating the loyalty and devotion of women in love, and their sufferings at the hands of men. In the 'retracciouns' that conclude the *Canterbury Tales*, Chaucer refers to the *Legend* as 'the book of the xxv. Ladies', but the text as we have it contains only nine stories, most of them drawn from Ovid, and featuring such victims of male treachery as Dido, Medea, Ariadne, and Philomel. The work breaks off in the middle of the ninth legend, either having lost its ending or never having been completed; Lydgate joked that Chaucer was unable to find enough good women to finish it.[34]

The puzzle for literary critics is the question of which bit of this literary drama to take seriously. If we take the apology enacted by the *Legend of Good Women* in earnest, does that mean that Chaucer is equally in earnest in suggesting that the *Troilus* has antifeminist implications? Or, if one thinks – as I do – that the *Troilus* is remarkable, given the nature of its story, for its *lack* of antifeminist feeling, does this mean that Chaucer is insincere in apologising for it in the *Legend*? There are indeed critics who would see this apology as a merely cynical charade, and who would read the ensuing narratives of betrayed and suffering women as either the mechanical execution of a literary commission imposed on Chaucer by the Queen or some other noble lady, or as deeply ironic, their professed sympathy denied by an underlying current of ridicule.[35]

If we look to the imitations of Chaucer's apologies to women in his literary followers, we might conclude that we

are in fact dealing with nothing more than a ritual convention, in which it would be foolish to look for sincerity, or for
any deeper sense of the reasons why an apology might be
called for. Lydgate, in particular, makes a positive habit of
apologising to women, while at the same time keeping up a
steady stream of antifeminist commonplaces.[36] In Book I of
the *Fall of Princes*, for example, where he is recycling a
French translation of a Latin work by Boccaccio, he reproduces a chapter in which Boccaccio is prompted by the story
of Delilah to make a violent attack on 'þe malis of wommen'
(6511–706: their major vice seems to be using make-up).
Boccaccio grudgingly ends his chapter with the acknowledgement that there *are* a few good women, who ought
of course to be given their due, but they are so rare that
it is safer to steer clear of the sex altogether; the French
translator follows him faithfully.[37] Lydgate turns this
third-person comment into a direct address to 'Ye women
all, that shal beholde & see / This chapitle and the processe
reede', urging them not to mind what Boccaccio says if
their virtue makes it inapplicable to them (1 6707–34).[38]
In Lydgate's *Troy Book*, where he is following the Latin
version of Benoît de Sainte-Maure produced by Guido delle
Colonne, he reproduces Guido's antifeminist comments –
not only the remarks on the treachery of Briseida/Criseyde
which Guido took over from Benoît, but also the hostile
comments on Medea and Helen for which Guido himself was
responsible.[39] But in each case Lydgate adds a routine
apology. The violent outburst against 'þe insaciate change
and mutabilite of women' which is provoked by nothing
more dreadful than Medea's falling in love with Jason is far
worse than anything in Guido, but he is made to bear the
blame for it:[40]

> Allas, whi wolde he so cursedly write
> Ageynes hem, or with hem debate!   (I 2098–9)

Lydgate protests that he is sorry to have to translate such stuff. Guido's attacks on Helen and Criseyde are similarly, as Derek Pearsall has noted, 'fallen upon with ... delight, expanded with much new material (II, 3531–631, III, 4264–417), and then repudiated with mock-outrage'.[41] In both cases Lydgate again blames Guido and claims that he is translating against his will, but gives the game away with ironic insertions in the apologies, asking, for example, à propos of Criseyde, why women should be blamed if they are *naturally* duplicitous (III 4407–8)? Similarly with Medea, he says it is only reasonable for women to take new lovers, since men do the same, and women have to look after their own interests (I 2108–14). 'And ȝif I koude I wolde hem excuse', says Lydgate, clearly echoing Chaucer's protestation that he would excuse Criseyde for pity if he could (*Troilus and Criseyde* v 1098–9).[42]

This, I think, is the key to Lydgate's combination of antifeminist material with a subsequent apology; this ritual combination of affirmation and denial is the nearest he can get to Chaucerian irony (Chaucerian *sincerity* is utterly beyond him).[43] Derek Pearsall puts it well when he says that Lydgate 'found in the conventional patterns of the anti-feminist dialogue the opportunity for a degree of complexity and irony and "suspension" in his account of human behaviour which he could rarely manage elsewhere ... What Lydgate actually thought of women is irrelevant: I doubt whether he thought much about them at all.'[44]

Pearsall calls Lydgate's apologies 'literary exercises',[45] and this view of them is confirmed by one of the manuscript selections from the *Fall of Princes* (MS London, British Library, Harley 2251), which uses the text as the material for just such a literary exercise; whoever composed it has carefully culled antifeminist stanzas from various parts of Lydgate's vast work, and re-composed them into a separate poem, ending with the apology to women which follows the Boccaccian attack.[46] A contemporary annotator (possibly, Tony Edwards suggests, the scribe himself) takes this carefully concocted opposition one stage further by adding indignant protests in the margins, in the manner of undergraduates writing in English Faculty library books: the antifeminist remarks provoke such replies as 'Holdith youre pees', 'be pees I bidde yow', 'Ye have no cause to say so', and so on. The final apology is rewarded with the grudging acknowledgement, 'There is no goode wommane that wilbe wroth ne take no quarell agenst this booke as I suppose.' The reminiscence of the Wife of Bath in the comment 'Be pees or i wil rende this leef out of youɪ book' raises suspicions of the factitious nature of this marginal indignation, but even if we see it as a spontaneous and sincere reaction on the part of some reader (rather than part of a little drama arranged by the scribe), it provides an indication, I think, of the cynical or lazy motives that could inspire Lydgate and others to go through their ritual yea-and-nay saying about women: it is an easy way to create a controversy that will attract interest, an easy way to win the reader's involvement.[47]

So one sometimes finds writers trying to create a controversial atmosphere for their works which will generate such involvement and interest, by apologising even when it is hard to see what there is to apologise about. Thomas Hoccleve, another of Chaucer's later admirers, offers a case in point. His long and rambling *Dialogue with a Friend* ends with the friend's suggestion that he should write something in praise of women, as a recompense for having traduced them in an earlier work.[48] Hoccleve defends himself, as Jean de Meun had done, by saying that he was 'noon Auctour' – not the originator of his material – but only 'a reportour / Of folkes tales'; 'as they seide / I wroot' (760–2). Whoever repeats 'a mannes sawe', says Hoccleve, must do so exactly, without changing it in any way (764–5). What is odd about all this is that the work for which Hoccleve is being held guilty is the *Epistle of Cupid*, which is not 'a mannes sawe' at all but a woman's; it is a translation and remodelling of Christine de Pisan's *Epistle to the God of Love*, which – as one would expect from Christine – rehearses antifeminist criticisms only in order to reject them with vigour and contempt.[49] Hoccleve does eventually get round to pointing out that the poem is really in women's favour, but he nevertheless concludes the *Dialogue* by asking pardon 'thogh I nat trespace' (816), in order, he says, to avoid 'open werre' with the ladies, and sets about relating the tale of a Roman Empress, a paragon of goodness, who preserves her virtue through all sorts of trials and hardships, by way of making amends.

Hoccleve is clearly trying to create a Chaucerian atmosphere in this apology: his claim that anyone who repeats 'a mannes sawe' must reproduce it accurately is an obvious echo of Chaucer's similar claim in the *General Prologue* to the *Canterbury Tales* (although the latter is not à propos of antifeminism but of 'brood' language). Hoccleve's Friend cites the Wife of Bath as authority for women's dislike of being criticised (694–7). And when Hoccleve tells the story of the Roman Empress, he interpolates occasional jocular comments, as Lydgate does, in a manner clearly meant to imitate Chaucerian irony. A eulogy of female constancy, for example, peters out in a concessive clause which undermines the praise (484–97), and the Emperor's final joy at being reunited with his wife after her harrowing adventures are over calls forth the comment that some men wouldn't have been so pleased to have their wives restored to them (939–45). Similarly, Lydgate comments on the story of Orpheus that some men would think themselves lucky to be able to get rid of their wives just by looking over their shoulders.[50] Neither Hoccleve nor Lydgate seems to have noticed that Chaucer's ironic asides characteristically jibe at *men*, rather than women – witness, for example, his sardonic comment in the *Man of Law's Tale* (a narrative of the same type as Hoccleve's story of the Empress), when his heroine Constance tearfully sets out to cross the sea at her father's command to marry the Sultan of Syria. What wonder if she wept, says Chaucer, at being sent to a distant country to be bound in 'subjeccioun' to an unknown husband?

> Housbondes been alle goode, and han ben yoore;
> That knowen wyves; I dar sey yow na moore.   (272–3)

When his irony does involve women, as in the long exhortation to 'noble wyves' at the end of the *Clerk's Tale*, which urges them on no account to imitate Griselda's patience but on the contrary to scold and bully their husbands continually, it is again not women but men who are the true target. The encouragement to female bullying comes as the result of and compensation for the male bullying shown in the tale, so that the antifeminist thrust of the irony is deflected by the context.[51]

A few years after Hoccleve wrote his *Dialogue* (c. 1421),[52] we find Alain Chartier, a poet at the French court, writing an *Excusacioun aux Dames* for his poem *La Belle Dame Sans Merci*.[53] Here too it is difficult to see what warrants apology; the *Belle Dame* is nothing more obnoxious than a debate between a lady and a young man who is in love with her, in which she persistently rejects his suit. The *Excusacioun* represents Alain's fault as having been to suggest that women could be devoid of pity; he is subjected to a mock indictment by some ladies of the court, and in the *Excusacioun* is threatened with punishment by the God of Love. The whole thing, as Professor Laidlaw suggests, seems to be no more than a literary – or courtly – game.[54]

The practice of writing an antifeminist (or allegedly antifeminist) work and following it up with a retraction predates the fifteenth century, however; we find it in the fourteenth, in some works that Chaucer very probably knew. In the 1370s a French writer called Jehan le Fèvre translated a virulently antifeminist work in Latin, the *Lamentations* of one Matheolus, a married cleric, who had learned to regret the curtailment of his career which resulted from his abandonment of celibacy.[55] Already in the translation itself, Jehan turns aside to excuse himself for the misogynistic nature of his material, and to protest that he bears no malice towards women (II 1541–70).[56] Like Lydgate, he claims he is only a translator, obliged to reproduce his source accurately (II 1560–5; cf. 2589–608).[57] This excuse might arouse some scepticism, since not only could he have chosen to translate some other text, if Matheolus was so repugnant to him, but also it appears that he frequently expands the antifeminist material of his original, adding new details of his own.[58] However he then followed up the translation of the *Lamentations* with a work of his own called the *Livre de Leesce* (Book of Joyfulness), which is a full-scale defence of women to match Matheolus's attacks on them. It opens with an apology to women for having slandered them, and the conventional defence that he was only translating (1–11). Jehan goes on to point out that all the exemplary tales of women's wickedness are nothing but pagan legends or low jokes (e.g., 739–9, 795–9, 810–12, 2697–706); he lists dozens of good women whose examples counterbalance the bad ones (2799–922); he provides evidence that women are braver than men (3528–617), wiser than men (3618–87), better at looking after plants and animals (3688–703), and more religious (3704–9). They bear children in pain and wear their fingers to the bone in household chores while their husbands idle away their time in the pub or out hunting (3742–75). The vigour and ingenuity of this defence testifies to a certain kind of commitment on Jehan's part, but one may wonder whether the *Livre de Leesce* was the easier to conceive because the *Lamentations* was not entirely serious in the first place. This is suggested, not only by the extremism of its polemic, but also by the content of Book III, in which Matheolus has a hostile interview with God, bitterly questioning him on why he made women or instituted marriage. God is rather sheepish under this attack, rehearsing his sufferings on behalf of mankind as if to say he has his troubles too (1467–82, 1550–84, 1663–71). He defends himself by saying that in order to correct sinners, he has made several purgatories, chief of which is marriage (1673–1710); the husband has only to suffer in patience and he will go straight to heaven when he dies (1711–20). Matheolus is finally vouchsafed a pseudo-Dantesque vision of heaven, in which he sees married men granted the same degree of bliss as the martyrs of

24

the Church, above bishops, monks and hermits (2762–4, 2775–86).

Jehan le Fèvre's two works confirm the view that writing against women and then apologising for it is as often as not just a convenient way of manufacturing a literary subject; neither activity is evidence of a seriously held view of women (this is not to say, of course, that such works didn't have serious *consequences*). So the fourteenth-century Anglo-Norman writer Nicole Bozon uses alleged objections to antifeminist remarks in his *Char d'Orgueil* as an excuse for writing a little poem on *La Bonté des Femmes*.[59] And Guillaume de Machaut spins his much longer *Judgement of the King of Navarre* out of an allegation that he has traduced women in the *Judgement of the King of Bohemia*.[60] Again, the offence is not obvious, since the earlier work is a debate between a lady whose lover has died, and a knight whose mistress has abandoned him for another, as to which of them suffers most. To anyone reading this poem it might seem that the major reason for female complaint is that the knight's long-windedness hardly allows the lady to get a word in edgeways, but what is objected to in the *Navarre* is that the final judgement is cast in the knight's favour, thus – it is alleged – undervaluing woman's suffering. The allegation against Machaut is made by 'a lady of great nobility', and Machaut agrees to argue the case of male versus female suffering all over again with a whole group of female personifications, such as Temperance, Peace, Faith, Constancy, Charity, and so on, in the presence of the king of Navarre. The debate itself takes the form of a story-telling contest, in which both sides produce tales (many of them, like those in Chaucer's *Legend*, drawn from Ovid) in support of their respective views. The king's decree goes against

Machaut, and it is determined that he should write three poems by way of atonement for his sins against the God of Love, whose service demands constant reverence for women.

There are obvious similarities here with the *Legend of Good Women*, and Chaucer very probably modelled his poem on Machaut's.[61] What unites them, as others have noted,[62] is not only the similarities of situation and content, but also a concern to dramatise the relationship between the poet and his poetry, to create a poetic personality which asserts its presence in the work and yet is challenged for control over it by the claims of the readers to whom it is addressed. Women become merely the pretext for a debate about literary authority.

If this is an accurate picture of Machaut's work, it does not in my view fully account for Chaucer's *Legend*, for several reasons. In the first place, the structure of Machaut's poem is designed to give him the starring role; the whole debate refers itself to him, and he is a strong presence throughout. In the Prologue to Chaucer's *Legend*, however, the poet's guilt is argued out between the God of Love and Alcestis, who takes his part. The effect of this is to re-instate woman in a leading role; it is Alcestis, not a male authority figure such as the king of Navarre, who determines Chaucer's fate. And when the narration of the legends themselves gets under way, the male poet keeps himself subordinate to his female subject. Secondly, Machaut's contributions to the debate on the strength of woman's feelings lead him into far blunter antifeminist remarks than anything to be found in the work for which he stands charged,[63] whereas Chaucer consistently sticks to the woman's point of view throughout the *Legend*. He not only repeatedly emphasises 'pitee' as the virtue women have and men notably lack, he also makes 'pitee' into the dominant response called for by these stories of female suffering, thus 'feminising' the reader, as it were, by the process of reading.[64] Last but not least, the 'lady of great nobility' who makes the accusation against Machaut, and for whom he claims to feel great reverence, disappointingly turns out to be not a real woman at all but another personification; her name is Bonneurté, meaning Happiness or Good Fortune (3851). *Real* women thus disappear from the poem.[65] In contrast, Chaucer, as we have seen, carefully makes reference in his Prologue to the effect the *Troilus* is likely to have had on real women. And his Ovidian stories are not, like Machaut's, simply sentimental narratives of love and death; they include the brutal rapes of Lucretia and Philomel, which confront the real crimes of men against women in their most serious form.

Machaut's subject defines itself as the poet's relation to his poetry; Chaucer's subject defines itself as the poet's responsibility to women. If the *Troilus* is not antifeminist, it is not necessary to conclude that the *Legend of Good Women* is cynical; the apology acknowledges the possibility of antifeminist *readings* of the *Troilus*, even despite its lack of antifeminist motivation. No writer can control the use made of the literary work by readers. Well before Christine de Pisan had cited the case of the woman who had to endure her husband's readings from the *Romance of the Rose*, Chaucer had spontaneously imagined such a woman in his picture of the Wife of Bath, whose fifth husband constantly torments her by reading aloud from a comprehensive anthology of antifeminist literature. Chaucer here places antifeminist material in a context that obliges us to take a woman's point of view on it, a context where it appears neither as a literary exercise nor a pleasant game but as an instrument of perpetual torture.

To demonstrate the seriousness of Chaucer's commitment to women would take far more than the few minutes I have left. It would require me to show, for example, how Chaucer patiently transforms the story of Criseyde so that her betrayal is evidence neither of female fickleness nor of female sensuality, but of a mutability ineradicably present in human nature as a whole. It would require me to show how in the *Canterbury Tales* it is women rather than men in whom he chooses to embody the values he admires; there are no male heroes to set against Constance, Griselda, Virginia, Prudence, Cecilia.[66] I have time only to take one last example from his works, the moment in the *Nun's Priest's Tale* where the apology to women is given its comic apotheosis, raised to such a pitch of absurdity that it is revealed as the empty ritual it is. The tale is the story of a cock and hen – a barnyard incident elevated by a mock heroic style into a drama of cosmic significance. Chauntecleer, the cock, is visited by a warning dream presaging his seizure by the fox. When he tells his wife Pertelote of the fear this dream has aroused in him, she is aghast to think she might be married to a coward. She insists the dream is merely the result of indigestion, and prescribes laxatives. Chauntecleer resists this suggestion with determination, and defends himself with a speech hundreds of lines long on the importance of dreams as true indicators of future events. Having won the argument, however, he declares that the beauty of her scarlet-red eyes makes him feel so wonderful that he is ready to defy his dream, and he pays no further attention to it. It turns out that he didn't need the dream

anyway, because when the fox finally turns up, Chauntecleer *instinctively* takes fright at it, since, as Chaucer carefully points out, beasts can recognise their natural enemies
even if they have never seen them before. The fox, however,
allays his fears and manages to persuade the cock by flattery
into giving a demonstration of his best crowing, standing on
tiptoes with his eyes closed so as to put maximum effort into
it. This gives the fox his chance to seize the cock and run
away with him. Anticipating this disaster, the narrator of
the tale pours forth a stream of rhetorical lamentation, with
much hand-wringing over destiny, free will, and the question of God's responsibility for catastrophe.[67] But, he concludes, such questions are not really for him to settle:

> My tale is of a cok, as ye may heere,
> That tok his conseil of his wyf, with sorwe,
> To walken in the yerd upon that morwe
> That he hadde met that dreem that I yow tolde.　　(3252–5)

This comment will strike the attentive reader as absurd,
since, as we have seen, Chauntecleer precisely did *not* take
his wife's advice but insisted on asserting the importance of
dreams in order to get out of taking laxatives. In any case, it
is not walking in the yard, but succumbing to the fox's
flattery, that causes his downfall; like January in the *Merchant's Tale* he falls victim to his own wilful blindness. The
same masculine blindness characterises the narrator's ener-
getic indictment of women as the cause not only of this
disaster but of disasters in general:

> Wommennes conseils been ful ofte colde;
> Wommannes conseil broghte us first to wo
> And made Adam fro Paradys to go,
> Ther as he was ful myrie and wel at ese.　　(3256–9)

29

This ritual accusation is followed by the ritual apology:

> But for I noot to whom it myght displese,
> If I conseil of wommen wolde blame,
> Passe over, for I seyde it in my game.
> Rede auctours, where they tret of swich mateere,
> And what they seyn of wommen ye may heere.
> Thise been the cokkes wordes, and nat myne;
> I kan noon harm of no womman divyne.   (3260–6)

'These are the cock's words ...'. The absurdity detectable earlier here becomes absolutely unmistakable. The traditional claim to be repeating another's words is turned into pure nonsense; what, in heaven's name, in all this farrago of rhetorical commentary, is supposed to have been uttered by the *cock*?[68] The apology, with its traditional appeal to other authors to bear the blame for antifeminist utterances, is revealed as merely a mechanical piece of rhetoric, an evasion of authorial responsibility, equivalent to the evasion of masculine responsibility in the antifeminist comments themselves, which try to pin the blame for the fox's actions on the hen.

Comedy here unmasks the ritual combination of antifeminism and apology and demonstrates its failure to connect with the real dynamics of events; it is merely part of a protective shield of rhetoric whose role is to save men from the necessity to think seriously about their own lives – easier just to blame it on God, on destiny, or on women. It is thus precisely the ridicule with which he invests this apology to women that testifies, paradoxically, to the seriousness of Chaucer's thinking about them, and what literature does to them, and that convinces me that he alone, of all the male writers I have instanced, has an idea of what a *real* apology to a woman would look like.

Notes

1 Having been in advance of Oxford in the establishment of women's colleges in the 1870s, Cambridge was consistently behind it in the progress towards admission of women to full membership of the university, which in Oxford was achieved in 1920. See Rita McWilliams-Tuberg, *Women at Cambridge: A Men's University – Though of a Mixed Type* (London, 1975).

2 On the dialogic nature of both reading and writing, see especially Tzvetan Todorov, *Mikhail Bakhtin: The Dialogical Principle*, trans. Wlad Godzich (Manchester, 1984).

3 Since I have recently encountered some misunderstanding of the term 'antifeminism' among non-medievalists, I had better make clear that medievalists have traditionally applied it to literary expressions of hostility to *women*, and not hostility to *feminism* (which would clearly be anachronistic).

4 'Carissime donne ... Sono adunque, discrete donne, ... stati alcuni che, queste novellette leggendo, hanno detto che voi mi piacete troppo e che onesta cosa non è che io tanto diletto prenda di piacervi e di consolarvi . . . di commendarvi, come io fo'; *Decameron*, ed Vittore Branca (Florence, 1965), pp. 449–50. All quotations from the *Decameron* are from this edition; translations are taken from *Giovanni Boccaccio: The Decameron*, trans. G. H. McWilliam (Harmondsworth, 1972).

5 'Deh! se vi cal di me, fate che noi ce ne meniamo una colà su di queste papere, e io le darò beccare' (ed. Branca, p. 455).

6 'Saranno per avventura alcune di voi che diranno che io abbia nello scriver queste novelle troppa licenzia usata, sì come in fare alcuna volta dire alle donne e molto spesso ascoltare cose non assai convenienti né a dire né ad ascoltare ad oneste donne. La qual cosa io nego, per ciò che niuna sì disonesta n'è, che, con onesti vocaboli dicendola, sì disdica ad alcuno: il che qui mi pare assai convenevolmente bene aver fatto' (ed. Branca, p. 1238).

7 'E se forse pure alcuna particella è in quelle, alcuna paroletta

più liberale che forse a spigolistra donna non si conviene, le quali più le parole pesano che'fatti e più d'apparer s'ingegnano che d'esser buone, dico che più non si dee a me esser disdetto d'averle scritte, che generalmente si disdica agli uomini e alle donne di dir tutto dì *foro* e *caviglia* e *mortaio* e *pestello* e *salsiccia* e *mortadello*, e tutto pieno di simiglianti cose' (ed. Branca, p. 1239). McWilliam's translation substitutes familiar English euphemisms for the last two items.

8 The documents that constitute the celebrated 'querelle de la *Rose*' have been edited (and the Latin texts provided with modern French translations) by Eric Hicks, *Le Débat sur le Roman de la Rose*, Bibliothèque du XVᵉ Siècle 43 (Paris, 1977). For an English translation, see *La Querelle de la Rose: Letters and Documents*, Joseph L. Baird and John R. Kane, North Carolina Studies in the Romance Languages and Literatures (Chapel Hill, 1978).

9 For Christine's objection to this passage of the *Roman*, see *Débat*, ed. Hicks, p. 13: 'sans faille, a mon avis, trop traicte deshonnestement en aucunes pars – et mesmement ou personnage que il claime Raison, laquelle nomme les secréz membres plainement par nom'. I cite the edition of the *Roman de la Rose* by Félix Lecoy, Classiques Français du Moyen Age, 3 vols. (Paris, 1966–70); for a translation see Charles Dahlberg, *The Romance of the Rose* (Hanover and London, 1971).

10 *The Trial of Lady Chatterley: Regina v. Penguin Books Limited*, ed. C. H. Rolph (Harmondsworth, 1961), p. 17.

11 '... entre vous qui belles filles avéz et bien les desiréz a entroduire a vie honneste, bailliéz leur, bailliez et queréz *Le Rommant de la Rose* pour apprendre a discerner le bien du mal – que dis je! mais le mal du bien! ... Et dont que fait a louer lecture qui n'osera estre leue ne parlee en propre forme a la table des roynes, des princesses et des vaillans preudefemmes – a qui covendroit couvrir la face de honte rougie?' (*Débat*, ed. Hicks, pp. 15, 20; cf. pp. 52, 56).

12 This might be seen as a variant of Alan of Lille's joke in

the De Planctu Naturae, where Nature shows the sort of schoolgirlish coyness that the Lover requires, announcing that maidenly modesty obliges her to use metaphor rather than plain terms in describing the sexual vices of mankind (viz., homosexuality): 'nolo ut prius plana uerborum planicie explanare proposita uel prophanis uerborum nouitatibus prophanare prophana, uerum pudenda aureis pudicorum uerborum faleris inaurare uariisque uenustorum dictorum coloribus inuestire ... Sed tamen aliquando, ut superius libauimus, quia *rebus de quibus loquimur cognatos oportet esse sermones*, rerum informitati locutionis debet deformitas conformari. In sequenti tamen tractatu, ne locutionis cacephaton lectorum offendat auditum uel in ore uirginali locum collocet turpitudo, predictis uiciorum monstris euphonia orationis uolo pallium elargiri' (ed. Nikolaus M. Häring (Spoleto, 1978), VIII [Pr. 4], 183–95). For an English translation of this work, see James J. Sheridan, *Alan of Lille: The Plaint of Nature* (Toronto, 1980).

13 This last jibe is repeated by Boccaccio in the passage quoted in n. 7 above.

14 '... je vous confesse que le nom ne fait la deshonnesteté de la chose, mais la chose fait le nom deshonneste. Pour ce, selon mon faible avis, en doit estre parlé sobrement – et non sans neccessité – pour fin d'aucun cas particulier, comme de maladie ou autre honneste neccessaire. Et si comme naturellement les mucierent noz premiers parens, devons faire en fait et en parole' (*Débat*, ed. Hicks, p. 14; cf. p. 51).

15 '... Rayson fist a l'Amant ainssy come se je parloie a une fame grosse ou a ung malade, et je luy ramentevoye pommes aigres ou poires nouvelles ou autre fruit, que luy fut bien apetisant et contraire, et je luy disoie que se il en mengoit, ce luy nuirroit moult. Vraiement je tiens que mieulx li souvendroit et plus luy aroit penetré en son appetit les choses nommees que la deffence faicte de non en mengier: et sert au propos que autrefois ay dit – et tu tant le repprens – que on ne doit ramentevoir a

33

nature humainne le pié dont elle cloche' (*Débat*, ed. Hicks, p. 125).

16 Gerson attributes this to man's fallen nature; just as a wine which would not harm a healthy man will have disastrous effects on a sick one, so it is that to see or hear of carnal matters openly will arouse base desires in sinners, although it would not have done so in the state of innocence (*Débat*, ed. Hicks, p. 84).

17 'Et que maistre Jehan de Meung ou chapistre de Raison ne descendi pas a parler des secrés membres pour affeccion qu'il y eust a en parler nuement et baudement, mais pour ce qu'il vint a propos et pour monstrer la folie a ceulx qui dient qu'il n'est licite d'en parler en nul cas par propres nons, appert par ce que ailleurs ou il parle de l'euvre de nature ne le nomme il pas par propre non (comme ou chapistre d'Ami et de la Vielle, esquelz il nomme le "jeu d'amours", la "besongne d'amours", et "ce tripot")' (*Débat*, ed. Hicks, p. 98).

18 'Il les nomme par mos poetiques entendables six fois plus atisans et plus penetratis et plus delicteus a ceulx qui y sont enclins que se il les nommast par leurs propres nons' (*Débat*, ed. Hicks, p. 125).

19 As noted by Maureen Quilligan, 'Words and Sex: The Language of Allegory in the *De planctu naturae*, the *Roman de la Rose*, and Book III of *The Faerie Queene*', *Allegorica* 2 (1977), 195–216, at p. 206.

20 'Words and Sex', p. 199; see also p. 206.

21 *The Scandal of the Fabliaux* (Chicago and London, 1986), p. 83.

22 'Ele n'oist parler de foutre / Ne de lecherie a nul fuer, / Que ele n'aüst mal au cuer . . .' (6–8): 'De la Damoisele qui ne pooit oir parler de foutre', *Nouveau Recueil Complet des Fabliaux*, vol. IV, ed. Willem Noomen and Nico van den Boogaard (Assen, 1988), pp. 57–89. My paraphrase follows the second of the two versions printed in this edition. See also Bloch's discussion of this fabliau, *Scandal*, pp. 87–9.

23 Quotations from Chaucer are taken from *The Riverside Chaucer*, 3rd edn, ed. Larry D. Benson (Boston, 1987).

24 The naivety is deftly exposed in Laurence Lipking's comment on 'the reluctance of literary men' in the eighteenth century 'to acknowledge the rights of women ... to plain speech, especially speech that mentions the naked facts of corporality. Women must be sheltered from a knowledge of what goes on beneath their clothes' (*Abandoned Women and Poetic Tradition* (Chicago and London, 1988), p. 78).

25 It is thus male lovers ('seigneur amoreus'), not women, whom Jean de Meun projects as the section of his audience likely to be offended by his use of broad language ('paroles / semblanz trop baudes ou trop foles': 15129–64); romantic gallantry and sexual titillation concur in the demand for euphemism.

26 Christine's disregard of narrative context is criticised by Jean de Montreuil (*Débat*, ed. Hicks, p. 42) and Pierre Col (ibid., p. 100). This argument is also reported by Gerson in his defence of Christine (ibid., p. 64).

27 '... je oÿ dire, n'a pas moult, a .i. de ces compaingnons de l'office dont tu es et que tu bien congnois, et homme d'auctorité, que il congnoit ung home marié, lequel ajouste foy au *Ronmant de la Rose* comme a l'Euvangile; celluy est souverainnement jaloux, et quant sa passion le tient plus aigrement il va querre son livre et list devant sa fame, et puis fiert et frappe sus et dist: "Orde, telle comme quelle il dist, voir que tu me fais tel tour. Ce bon sage homme maistre Jehan de Meung savoit bien que femmes savoient fere!" Et a chascun mot qu'il treuve a son propos il fiert ung coup ou deux du pié ou de la paume; si m'est advis que quiconques s'en loe, telle povre famme le compere chier' (*Débat*, ed. Hicks, pp. 139–40).

28 Piere Col, however, took the apology at face value (*Débat*, ed. Hicks, p. 110).

29 I cite the edition of Léopold Constans, Société des Anciens Textes Français, 6 vols. (Paris, 1904–12). I am grateful to Roberta Krueger for drawing my attention to this apology, and

thus setting me off on the line of enquiry that resulted in this lecture.

30 See Penny Eley, 'Author and Audience in the *Roman de Troie*', pp. 179–90 in *Courtly Literature: Culture and Context*, ed. Keith Busby and Erik Kooper (Amsterdam and Philadelphia, 1990).

31 This desire to enliven the narrative by involving the audience seems the likely motive behind Ariosto's apology for Ruggiero's sudden departure from Bradamante, which he fears his female readers may find ungallant – yet, he says, any women who truly loved would recognise the over-riding claims of honour (*Orlando Furioso* XXXVIII 1–3).

32 'Giovane donna, e mobile e vogliosa / È negli amanti molti'; *Filostrato* VIII 30, ed. Vittore Branca, in *Giovanni Boccaccio: Tutte le Opere*, vol. II (Milan, 1964). For an English translation, see the parallel text of the *Filostrato* edited and translated by Nathaniel Edward Griffin and Arthur Beckwith Myrick (New York, 1978).

33 One such reason is his perception of the tragic irony that it is the very compliancy that men value in women (their 'pitee') that makes betrayal easier; another is that if it is the woman who is unfaithful, it is the man who is left in the traditionally 'female' position of impotent lamentation, so that the stereotypes of male activity and female helplessness are reversed rather than confirmed. On this see my *Geoffrey Chaucer* (Hemel Hempstead, 1991), pp. 29–31, 168–70.

34 *Fall of Princes* Prol. 330–6; cf. I 1795–1806. The edition cited is by Henry Bergen, 4 vols, EETS e.s. 121–4 (London, 1924–7; repr. 1967).

35 Robert Worth Frank, Jr, discusses and rejects the theory that Chaucer was bored with the work: *Chaucer and the Legend of Good Women* (Cambridge, Mass., 1972), pp. 189–210. For a summary of sides taken in the debate on whether the *Legend* is ironic or not, see Lisa J. Kiser, *Telling Classical Tales: Chaucer and the Legend of Good Women* (Ithaca, N.Y., and London, 1983), p. 21, n. 6. Recent attempts to resolve the question by more

complicated accounts of the poem fail to convince: Elaine Tuttle Hansen, 'Irony and the Antifeminist Narrator in Chaucer's *Legend of Good Women*', *Journal of English and Germanic Philology* 82 (1983), 11–31, argues that there is irony, but it is directed not at women, but at Cupid and the narrator of the poem, whose idealisation of women unwittingly supports the antifeminist tradition; Janet M. Cowen, 'Chaucer's *Legend of Good Women*: Structure and Tone', *Studies in Philology* 82 (1985), 416–36, suggests that the work is 'neither pure pathos nor pure satire', but encompasses both. For a fuller outline of my own view, see *Geoffrey Chaucer*, pp. 32–9.

36 Derek Pearsall, *John Lydgate* (London, 1970), p. 236, notes the 'continual running-fire kept up against women' in the *Fall of Princes* and the *Troy Book*, which is often expressed through heavy irony; for example, after reproducing Boccaccio's attack on women's vices, à propos of Phaedra, he adds the assurance that of course it is only *Cretan* women who are meant – English women are completely free of duplicity, fickleness and rebelliousness, and suffer patiently, at least 'whil no man doth hem greve' (*Fall of Princes* I 4719–53).

37 Giovanni Boccaccio, *De Casibus Illustrium Virorum. A Facsimile Reproduction of the Paris Edition of 1520*, introduced by Louis Brewer Hall (Gainesville, Florida, 1962), pp. 46–8 (Book I, ff. xiv–xiiv); Laurent de Premierfait, *Des Cas des Nobles Hommes et Femmes, Book I*, ed. Patricia May Gathercole, University of North Carolina Studies in the Romance Languages and Literatures 74 (Chapel Hill, 1968), Chapter XVIII (pp. 208–16).

38 The assumption that 'good women' will refuse to take offence at what is said of their sex is found elsewhere: Simon Gaunt has drawn my attention to the apology in Heldris de Cornouaille's *Roman de Silence* (thirteenth century), where he suggests that no good woman will mind his criticism of Eufeme, since he has also spoken well of Silence (*Le Roman de Silence*, ed. Lewis Thorpe (Cambridge, 1972), 6695–8).

39 I cite the edition of the *Troy Book* by Henry Bergen, EETS e.s.

97, 103, 106, 126, 4 vols. (London, 1906–35; repr. in 3 vols., 1973). Cf. Guido de Columnis, *Historia Destructionis Troiae*, ed. Nathaniel Edward Griffin (Cambridge, Mass., 1936), p. 164 (Briseida); p. 17 (Medea); pp. 70–1 (Helen).

40 Guido's comments are directed much more against Medea's father, and his folly in allowing his daughter contact with a man, than against Medea herself.

41 Pearsall, *John Lydgate*, p. 134.

42 Lydgate seems not to have known Benoît's *Roman de Troie* directly (Pearsall, *John Lydgate*, p. 125), and thus his own apologies are more likely to have been modelled on Chaucer's than on Benoît's apology to the 'riche dame'.

43 Similarly, as Pearsall notes (*John Lydgate*, p. 238), the envoy to widows which Lydgate adds to the story of Dido (*Fall of Princes* II 2199–33), advising them on no account to copy Dido's fidelity to her dead husband, but instead to provide themselves with new lovers, is clearly intended as an imitation to the Envoy of Chaucer's *Clerk's Tale*. His expansion of Guido's passing comment on Briseida, 'tamquam varia et mutabilis, sicut est proprium mulierum' (ed. Griffin, p. 198) into nearly thirty lines of ironic admiration for the 'pite' and 'routhe' that prompt women to take new lovers without delay (*Troy Book* IV 2148–77), likewise imitates Chaucer's ironic comment on May's 'pitee' for Damian in the *Merchant's Tale* (1986–95).

44 *John Lydgate*, p. 238; cf. pp. 135–6. See further A. S. G. Edwards, 'Lydgate's Attitudes to Women', *English Studies* 51 (1970), 436–7, suggesting that these attitudes were probably conditioned by occasion.

45 *John Lydgate*, p. 157, n. 24.

46 The composite text has been edited by A. S. G. Edwards, 'John Lydgate, Medieval Antifeminism and Harley 2251', *Annuale Mediaevale* 13 (1972), 32–44.

47 Similarly, the passages about women in the *Troy Book* provoke, as Pearsall points out, more marginal annotation in the manuscripts than any others (*John Lydgate*, p. 136).

48 The *Dialogue* is included in *Hoccleve's Works: The Minor Poems*, ed. Frederick J. Furnivall and I. Gollancz, EETS e.s. 61 and 73, rev. Jerome Mitchell and A. I. Doyle and repr. in one volume (London, 1970).

49 This has been pointed out by John V. Fleming, 'Hoccleve's "Letter of Cupid" and the "Quarrel" over the *Roman de la Rose*', *Medium Aevum* 40 (1971), 21–40. In the light of the parallels between this instance and the others I cite where the original work which is being objected to or repented of hardly qualifies as antifeminist, I am not convinced by Fleming's ingenious argument that the inappropriateness of the accusation is designed by Hoccleve to ridicule Christine de Pisan's failure to understand Jean de Meun; but I agree with him that in using a mock-accusation to generate a new work, Hoccleve is imitating Chaucer. It should also be noted that the *Epistle to Cupid* was written twenty years earlier than the *Dialogue* (see p. xxiii of the Introduction to *Minor Poems*, ed. Furnivall and Gollancz), so that readers of the later poem might have only a hazy memory of it.

50 *Fall of Princes* I 5804–17.

51 See further my *Geoffrey Chaucer*, pp. 151–2.

52 See pp. xxii–xxiii of the Introduction to *Minor Poems*, ed. Furnivall and Gollancz.

53 Both poems are edited by J. C. Laidlaw in *The Poetical Works of Alain Chartier* (Cambridge, 1974). The *Belle Dame Sans Merci* and the *Excusacioun* are dated to 1424 and 1425 respectively (see Laidlaw's introduction, pp. 7–8, 39–40). The *Belle Dame* (but not the *Excusacioun*) was translated into English by Sir Richard Roos; see *Political, Religious and Love Poems*, ed. Frederick J. Furnivall, EETS o.s. 15 (London, 1866, rev. 1903), pp. 80–111.

54 See Laidlaw's introduction, p. 8.

55 The Latin original, Jehan le Fèvre's translation, and Jehan's *Livre de Leesce* (see below) are edited by A.-G. van Hamel, *Les Lamentations de Matheolus et le Livre de Leesce de Jehan le Fèvre*,

de Resson, 2 vols., Bibliothèque de l'Ecole des Hautes Etudes 95–6 (Paris, 1892–1905). Van Hamel dates Matheolus's work to between 1295 and 1301 (II, Introduction, pp. CXIX–CXXVII). Internal evidence suggests that Jehan composed his *Livre de Leesce* towards the end of 1373 (ibid., pp. CLXXIX–CLXXXII), and van Hamel thinks it probable therefore that his translation of the *Lamentations* was made in 1371/2 (ibid., p. CLXXXII).

56 Similarly, one of the commentators on Walter Map's *Dissuasio Valerii ad Rufinum de non ducenda uxore*, one of the most widely circulated antifeminist pieces of the Middle Ages, inserts into his commentary a paragraph in which he dissociates himself from Valerius's low opinion of women, points out that he has written an 'opusculum' in their favour, and humbly asks God, the blessed Virgin and all the female saints to excuse him for what he has written (MS Oxford, University College 61, f. 21ᵛ; mid fourteenth-century). See Ruth J. Dean, 'Unnoticed Commentaries on the *Dissuasio Valerii* of Walter Map', *Mediaeval and Renaissance Studies* 2 (1950), 128–50, at pp. 145–6.

57 Jehan's version of the *Lamentations* is strongly influenced by the *Roman de la Rose*, and as van Hamel notes (II, Introduction, p. CXCII), his apology imitates Jean de Meun's (see p. 13 above) in shifting the blame for antifeminism on to the written authorities which have acted as 'evidence' for its truth.

58 For example, in the instances of female enslavement to sexual passion which follow immediately on his apology, it is Jehan who adds the daughters of Lot to Matheolus's list, and who also expands Matheolus's two lines on Phyllis and Dido into much fuller accounts of their 'unbridled sexuality' ('luxure desordenée'); II 1619–20, 1635–60. Van Hamel considers the possibility that the Latin text of the *Lamentations* from which Jehan was working was fuller than the version we now have, but accepts that he also made amplifications and additions to it (II, Introduction, pp. LIV–LXIV). Occasionally, however, Jehan abbreviates, omits, or tones down the antifeminist material of his original (ibid., pp. LXIV–LXV); he omits, for example, Matheo-

lus's lines (1532–9) on female fickleness (which should come after II 2191 in the French version), including the famous Vergilian dictum 'Varium et mutabile semper / Femina'.

59 The poem is printed in the Introduction to Bozon's *Contes moralisés*, ed. Lucy Toulmin-Smith and Paul Meyer, Société des Anciens Textes Français (Paris, 1889), pp. xxxII–xLI. The same manuscript contains another poem by Bozon comparing women to a magpie, which, as the editors note (p. xLI), is much more insulting to the sex than the stanzas in the *Char d'Orgueil* for which he claims to apologise in the *Bonté des femmes*. The easy co-existence of the two poems in the same manuscript indicates the entirely conventional nature of both antifeminism and apology.

60 Both works have been edited and translated by R. Barton Palmer (New York and London, 1984 (*Bohemia*) and 1988 (*Navarre*)). The *Jugement du Roi de Behaingne* was written before 1342; the earliest possible date for the *Jugement du Roi de Navarre* is November 1349 (see Palmer's Introduction to *Navarre*, p. xlvii).

61 See Palmer's Introduction to *Navarre*, pp. xliii–xlvi. As will become apparent, I disagree with Palmer's view that 'Chaucer's handling of this inherited material is more conservative, less audacious [than Machaut's]' (p. xlvi).

62 See William Calin, 'Machaut's Legacy: The Chaucerian Inheritance Reconsidered', *Studies in the Literary Imagination* 20 (1987), 9–22, esp. p. 14: 'the greatest gift Machaut offers Chaucer is the notion of a poet writing poetry about the writing of poetry by a poet'; see also Palmer's Introduction to *Navarre*, pp. xxix–xxxix.

63   Il est certein – et je l'afferme –
             Qu'en cuer de femme n'a riens ferme,
             Rien seür, rien d'estableté.
             Fors toute variableté.
             Et puis qu'elle est si variable
             Qu'elle en rien n'est ferme n'estable

41

Et que de petit se varie.
Il faut que de po pleure et rie.
Dont grant joie et grant tourment
N'i puelent estre longuement,
Car sa nature li enseingne,
Que tost rie et de po se pleingne;
Tost ottroie, tost escondit;
Elle a son dit et son desdit,
Et s'oublie enterinement
Ce que ne voit, legierement ...   (3019–34)

This female fickleness is contrasted with the firm reliability of
the male heart, which is 'fermes et seürs, / Sages, esprouvez, et
meürs, / Vertüeus et fors pour durer, / Et humbles pour mal
endurer ...' (3047–50).

64 See my *Geoffrey Chaucer*, pp. 39–43.

65 Similarly, the tale of the Emperor Jereslaus's wife which is told
   by Hoccleve to exemplify female virtue (see p. 21 above) is at its
   conclusion 'moralised' by Hoccleve's Friend so that the wife
   becomes the soul, subjected to the trials of the flesh (*Minor
   Poems*, pp. 175–8). Again women disappear as a real subject.

66 For a full elaboration of these points, see my *Geoffrey Chaucer*.

67 I say 'the narrator', rather than 'the Nun's Priest' or 'Chaucer',
   in order to make the point that it is not the antifeminism of an
   individual speaker which is at issue here; antifeminism and the
   ritual apology are embedded in the discourse of narrative
   alongside its other rhetorical strategies, and it is this traditional
   rhetorical discourse, rather than an individual person's attitudes, that is the subject of comedy in this tale.

68 I am not fully convinced of the presence of a pun on the sexual
   sense of 'cock' here, but lest it should be thought I have not
   considered it, I will record that it is at least possible; see
   Lorrayne Y. Baird, '*O.E.D.* Cock 20: The Limits of Lexicography
   of Slang', *Maledicta* 5 (1981), 213–25, and the early fifteenth-
   century lyric 'I have a gentle cock' (*Middle English Lyrics*, ed. R.

T. Davies (London, 1963), No. 64), which combines linguistic reminiscences of the *Nun's Priest's Tale* with sexual innuendo ('And every night he percheth him / In mine ladye's chaumber').